We Can Do It!
HELPING A FRIEND

By Lois Fortuna

Please visit our website, www.garethstevens.com. For a free color catalog of all our high-quality books, call toll free 1-800-542-2595 or fax 1-877-542-2596.

Library of Congress Cataloging-in-Publication Data

Fortuna, Lois, author.
 Helping a friend / Lois Fortuna.
     pages cm. — (We can do it!)
 Includes index.
 ISBN 978-1-4824-3807-9 (pbk.)
 ISBN 978-1-4824-3808-6 (6 pack)
 ISBN 978-1-4824-3809-3 (library binding)
 1. Helping behavior in children—Juvenile literature. 2. Friendship in children—Juvenile literature. I. Title.
 BF723.H45F67 2016
 177'.62—dc23
                                           2015028845

First Edition

Published in 2016 by
Gareth Stevens Publishing
111 East 14th Street, Suite 349
New York, NY 10003

Copyright © 2016 Gareth Stevens Publishing

Editor: Ryan Nagelhout
Designer: Laura Bowen

Photo credits: Cover, pp. 1, 5, 9 Monkey Business Images/Shutterstock.com; p. 7 MANDY GODBEHEAR/Shutterstock.com; p. 11 Arthur Tilley/Photolibrary/Getty Images; p. 13 SW Productions/Photodisc/Getty Images; p. 15 Pressmaster/Shutterstock.com; p. 17 Blend Images - Kidstock/Brand X Pictures/Getty Images; p. 19 Agnieszka Kirinicjanow/E+/Getty Images; p. 21 Katja Zimmermann/Taxi/Getty Images; p. 23 Brocreative/Shutterstock.com.

All rights reserved. No part of this book may be reproduced in any form without permission in writing from the publisher, except by a reviewer.

Printed in the United States of America

CPSIA compliance information: Batch #CW16GS: For further information contact Gareth Stevens, New York, New York at 1-800-542-2595.

Contents

Fun Friends.............4

The Lost Cat...........10

Homework Time......16

Cleaning Up...........18

Words to Know.......24

Index....................24

I have good friends.

We love to help out!

My friend Jason helps.
He pushes Sarah
on a swing.

My friend Dan lost his cat.
We help him find her!

My friend Nathan
needs help.
I help him learn to read.

Friends always need help.
Try to help your friends.

Help them
with their homework.

Help them clean up your neighborhood!

Friends can help you stay safe.

Always walk home with a friend.

Words to Know

 cat

 swing

Index

cat 10
homework 16

neighborhood 18
swing 8